W9-AHH-005

A Bird Watcher's Guide to
WRENS

By

Grace Elora

Gareth Stevens
PUBLISHING

Please visit our website, www.garethstevens.com. For a free color catalog of all our high-quality books, call toll free 1-800-542-2595 or fax 1-877-542-2596.

Cataloging-in-Publication Data

Names: Elora, Grace.
Title: A bird watcher's guide to wrens / Grace Elora.
Description: New York : Gareth Stevens Publishing, 2018. | Series: Backyard bird watchers | Includes index.
Identifiers: ISBN 9781538203491 (pbk.) | ISBN 9781538203514 (library bound) | ISBN 9781538203507 (6 pack)
Subjects: LCSH: Bird watching–Juvenile literature. | Birds–Identification–Juvenile literature. | Birds–Juvenile literature.
Classification: LCC QL677.5 E46 2018 | DDC 598.072'34–dc23

First Edition

Published in 2018 by
Gareth Stevens Publishing
111 East 14th Street, Suite 349
New York, NY 10003

Copyright © 2018 Gareth Stevens Publishing

Designer: Laura Bowen
Editor: Therese Shea

Photo credits: Cover, p. 1 (wren) Bonnie Taylor Barry/Shutterstock.com; cover, pp. 1–32 (paper texture) javarman/Shutterstock.com; cover, pp. 1–32 (footprints) pio3/Shutterstock.com; pp. 4–29 (note paper) totallyPic.com/Shutterstock.com; pp. 4–29 (photo frame, tape) mtkang/Shutterstock.com; p. 4 Feng Yu/Shutterstock.com; p. 5 Jim Craigmyle/Corbis/Getty Images; p. 7 (Bewick's) Ser Amantio di Nicolao/Wikimedia Commons; p. 7 (cactus) Flickr upload bot/Wikimedia Commons; p. 7 (Carolina) The Photographer/Wikimedia Commons; p. 7 (rock) Tm/Wikimedia Commons; p. 7 (house) Josve05a/Wikimedia Commons; p. 8 J. Esteban Berrio/Shutterstock.com; p. 9 (wren) Brian E Kushner/Shutterstock.com; p. 11 Michael Woodruff/Shutterstock.com; p. 13 John E Heintz Jr/Shutterstock.com; p. 15 Gerald Marella/Shutterstock.com; p. 17 Stephanie Frey/Shutterstock.com; p. 18 LorraineHudgins/Shutterstock.com; p. 19 (fox) Miroslav Hlavko/Shutterstock.com; p. 19 (opossum) Lisa Hagan/Shutterstock.com; p. 19 (raccoon) Ng Sai Kit/Shutterstock.com; p. 19 (cat) threewhitecats/Shutterstock.com; p. 20 Tom Reichner/Shutterstock.com; p. 21 Richard R Hansen/Science Source/Getty Images; pp. 23, 25 (inset) Steve Byland/Shutterstock.com; p. 25 (main) Amadeu Ito/Shutterstock.com; p. 27 (top) Joe McDonald/Corbis Documentary/Getty Images; p. 27 (bottom) Huaykwang/Shutterstock.com; p. 29 Elena Elisseeva/Shutterstock.com.

Printed in the United States of America

CPSIA compliance information: Batch #CS17GS: For further information contact Gareth Stevens, New York, New York at 1-800-542-2595.

CONTENTS

Words in the glossary appear in **bold** type the first time they are used in the text.

BE A BIRDER

My name's Cam, but everyone in my family calls me "Birdie." They started calling me that when I was a baby. It still fits because I love birds. We all do! We're a family of birders. A birder is a bird watcher. Watching birds is a great hobby. It can be really exciting, too!

I've been learning about the birds in my backyard called wrens. Read my journal. I bet you'll learn some fun things about them!

Bird-watching is a great way to spend time outdoors. We go to beautiful parks and nature preserves.

5

NOW YOU SEE THEM...

HOW TO RECOGNIZE A WREN

- size
- coloring and markings
- beak length
- tail length and shape

We've been seeing a lot of wrens in our yard lately, or rather catching a quick look. They're superfast little birds! There are many kinds of wrens, so we're trying to find out which kind the birds in our yard are. They all look the same, so they're likely the same **species**.

Since they're so fast, Grandpa took a photo. We can compare the photo to photos of wrens we find online. It's much easier than trying to remember what the birds look like!

Bewick's wren

rock wren

house wren

Grandpa's photo!

cactus wren

Carolina wren

7

THEY'RE HOUSE WRENS!

The wrens in our yard are called house wrens! They're very common. Each is about 5 inches (13 cm) long. These birds have a round, little body with short wings and a long tail. Their wings are darker brown than the rest of their body.

House wrens are found in most of North America at least part of the year. Check out the map on the next page. Where I live, it gets cold in winter, so house wrens **migrate** south.

House wrens may look a bit different from each other, but most look like this one.

HOUSE WREN RANGE MAP

North America

year round
summer
winter

9

SING ME A SONG

House wrens don't look fancy. They don't have bright feathers like cardinals or blue jays. However, they're some of the best singers of any bird. Both males and females sing, but males sing a lot more when they're looking for a **mate**.

When male and female house wrens pair up, the female sings to answer her mate. She makes a squealing sound that's different than the male's sounds. The male sometimes sings without opening his mouth! This is called a "whispering song."

Birdcalls are sounds that birds make to drive off enemies or to communicate ideas, such as where they are.

11

WHICH ONE?

Before a female chooses a mate, the male shows her several nesting places. Males make a few nests in a territory. A nest might be in a hole in a tree, an opening in a building, or a flowerpot. The nest is usually in a place with walls, so the birds feel safe.

After the male begins a nest in places like these, the female chooses one. Then she finishes it, using **twigs** and softer matter such as plants, grass, hair, and feathers.

We built this nest box to give the wrens a good place to build their nest. They chose it!

13

TOUGH BIRDS!

SO LIGHT!

A house wren weighs about the same as two quarters!

Because nest locations are so important, house wrens will do anything to get a good one—even if other birds are already using it! House wrens battle birds such as chickadees and bluebirds as well as other house wrens for nests.

Male house wrens will attack other birds to win a nesting spot they want, even if those birds are bigger. They'll poke holes in their eggs or push eggs out of the nest to get birds to go away. That's really mean!

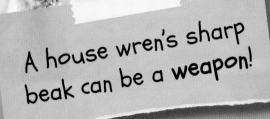

A house wren's sharp beak can be a weapon!

15

INTERESTING EGGS

A Bird Word

"Incubation" might sound like a hard word, but it just means sitting on eggs to keep them warm!

I wonder how many baby wrens we'll see in our backyard. A female wren may lay three to 10 eggs at a time. The eggs are white, but look different than the chicken eggs we eat. They're small, less than 1 inch (2.5 cm) long. They also have reddish brown dots on them.

The female sits on the eggs to keep them warm. It's important that the eggs don't get too cold, or they won't **hatch**.

This isn't a picture of our nest box because I don't want to scare the birds. This is what house wren eggs look like.

17

FIGHTING BACK

Out of the Air

Sometimes, owls and hawks catch house wrens while they're flying! Yikes!

18

I saw the neighbor's cat sitting under the nesting box. Cats are bird predators! Predators are animals that try to eat other animals. House wrens have many enemies, including cats, rats, opossums, woodpeckers, foxes, owls, hawks, raccoons, squirrels, and snakes.

We have a lot of squirrels and cats in my neighborhood. The house wrens don't seem scared. They sometimes chase predators or even hit them. That's pretty brave for a little bird!

I'd be scared of something that was trying to eat me!

FEED ME!

20

More, More!

Wren parents may feed babies 30 times an hour—or more!

The mother wren sits on her eggs for 12 to 15 days. When the eggs hatch, the chicks are almost naked. They have a few feathers on them, but not enough to keep them warm. Their eyes are closed, too! They won't leave the nest for around 2 weeks.

Both wren parents feed the chicks in the nest. The chicks, called nestlings, keep their parents very busy. They always want to eat! They grow very fast.

Look how cute
the chicks are!

21

TASTY TREATS?

I couldn't see what the wren parents were feeding the nestlings, so I looked it up online. Bugs are house wrens' favorite food, including beetles, grasshoppers, crickets, caterpillars, moths, flies, and spiders. Eating these creepy-crawlies sounds gross to me, but a wren wouldn't like what I eat, either!

House wrens sometimes eat snails, too. They even eat snail shells! The hard shells give them **nutrients** and help break down other food in their stomach.

This wren looks like it's really enjoying its meal!

23

HELLO, FLEDGLINGS!

Today, I finally saw the nestlings leave the nest. I counted four little wrens! They had some feathers, but their feathers don't look the same as adult wrens'. They have a smaller tail, too. They were ready to fly . . . kind of. They looked **clumsy**! Wrens that are starting to fly are called fledglings. They don't usually go back to the nest once they leave.

Some father wrens don't stay to help the fledglings. They might fly away to have another family. This father stayed!

Oldest Known
House Wren
9 years old

fledgling

adult

You can see that a fledgling's feathers look different than an adult house wren's feathers.

25

COME BACK!

It's getting colder out. Most house wrens migrate, so I've said good-bye to ours. I can put on a coat to keep warm, but they can't! They fly south. Maybe I'll see them when I visit Grandma in Florida in January.

Some house wrens return to the same area in the spring, but others move to new places. Young male house wrens may move to a territory close to an older male wren to watch how he finds nesting spots.

Will these house wrens come back in the spring? I hope so!

27

USEFUL BIRDS

Cleaning House?

Some people clean out their nesting boxes when the birds leave. Leaving a nest might make house wrens want to use the box again, though.

I've learned that house wrens are cute and tough. They're also helpful to people. That's because they eat bugs that people think are pests, such as beetles and caterpillars. These bugs eat people's plants. Mom wouldn't like them eating the plants in her garden!

Now that the house wrens are gone, I'll look for another kind of bird to watch. There are plenty that stick around for winter. They'll need me to keep the bird feeder full!

There are always new birds to learn about!

29

GLOSSARY

binoculars: a tool that you hold up to your eyes and look through to see things that are far away

clumsy: doing something in an uneasy way

communicate: to give or receive information through noise, writing, or movement

hatch: to break out of an egg

mate: one of two animals that come together to make babies

migrate: to move from one area to another for a season

nutrient: something that plants, animals, and people need to live and grow

parasite: an animal or plant that lives in or on another animal or plant and gets food or shelter from it

preserve: an area where plants, animals, or minerals are guarded

species: a group of animals that are alike and can produce young animals

twig: a small branch

weapon: something that is used for fighting, attacking, or defense

FOR MORE INFORMATION

Books

Burnie, David. *Bird-Watcher*. New York, NY: DK Publishing, 2015.

Cate, Annette. *Look Up! Bird-Watching in Your Own Backyard*. Somerville, MA: Candlewick Press, 2013.

Gillespie, Katie. *Birds*. New York, NY: AV2 by Weigl, 2013.

Websites

House Wren
www.allaboutbirds.org/guide/House_Wren/lifehistory
Many more facts about the house wren can be found here.

House Wren
www.audubon.org/field-guide/bird/house-wren
Check out the pretty songs and calls of the house wren.

INDEX